CAMBRIDGE

GREENMAN
& THE
MAGIC FOREST

B

Marilyn Miller

Teacher's Resource Book

Karen Elliott

T0349623

Contents

1 The Surprise

| get up | get dressed | wash your face | brush your teeth | brush your hair | have breakfast |

Trace to find the surprise.

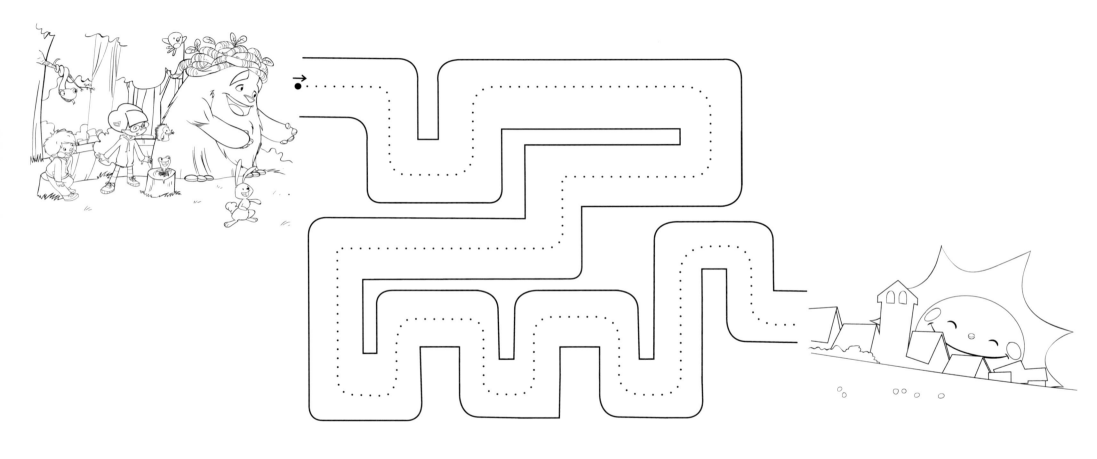

Trace and colour.

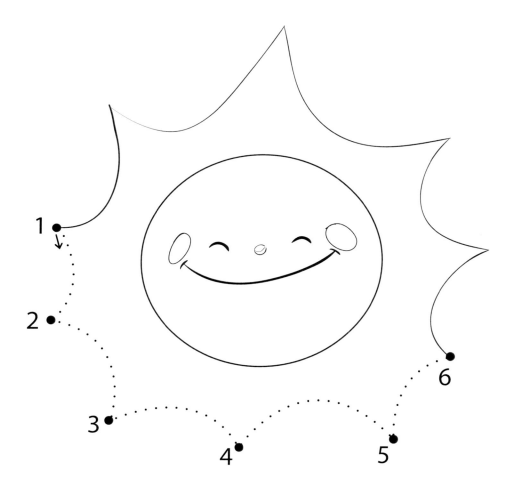

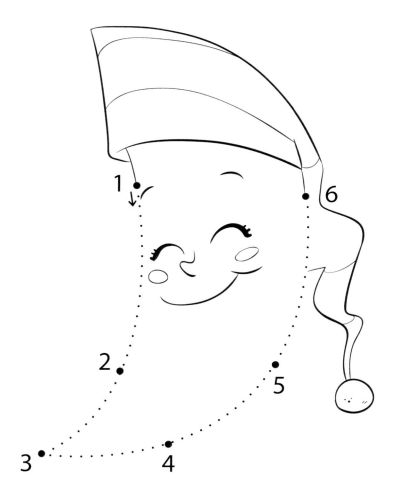

Cut out the pictures and words.

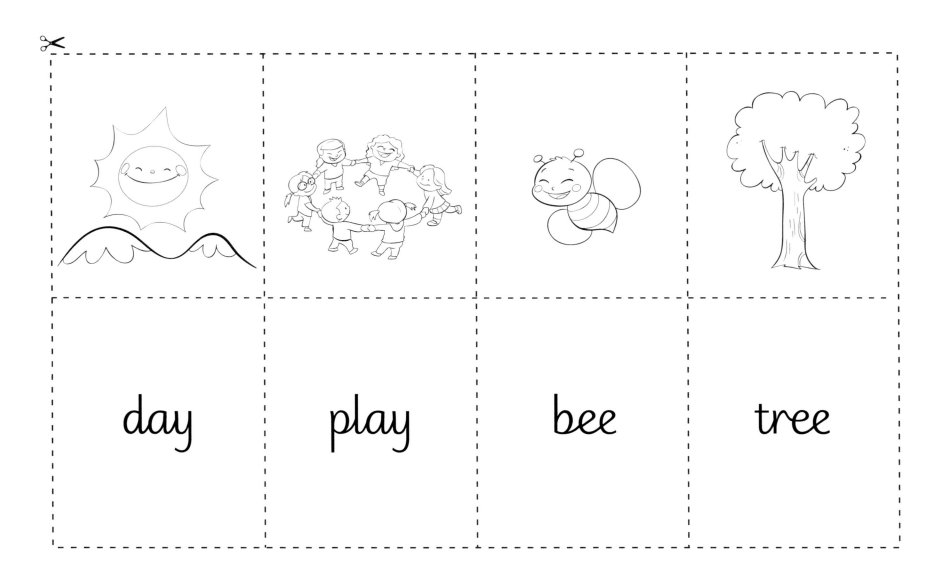

day   play   bee   tree

2 The Brown Mouse

Match and trace.

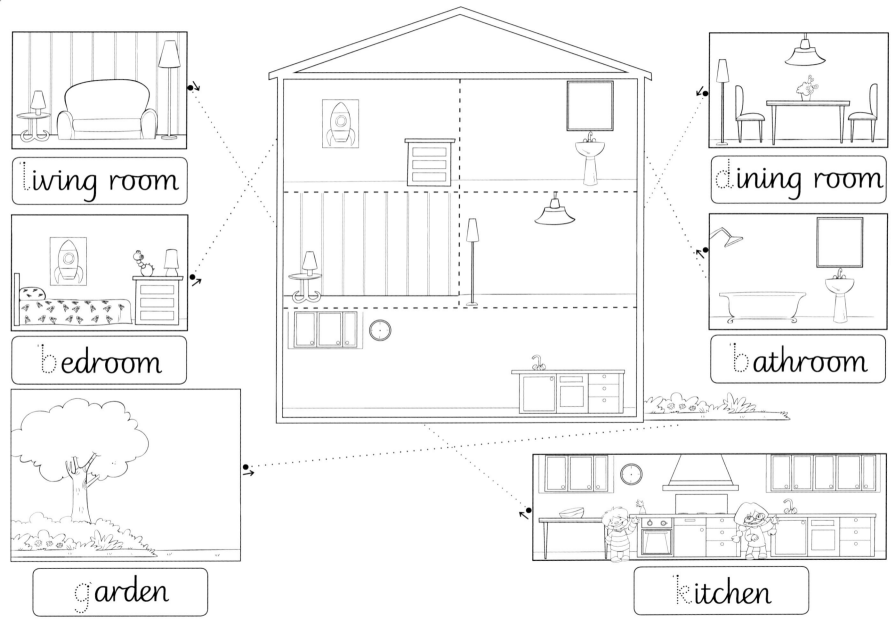

living room

bedroom

garden

dining room

bathroom

kitchen

Find the 5 differences. Then colour Sam.

■ **Value: helping**

Greenman and the Magic Forest B © Cambridge University Press. **Photocopiable 6**

Help the cat find the six mice and colour.

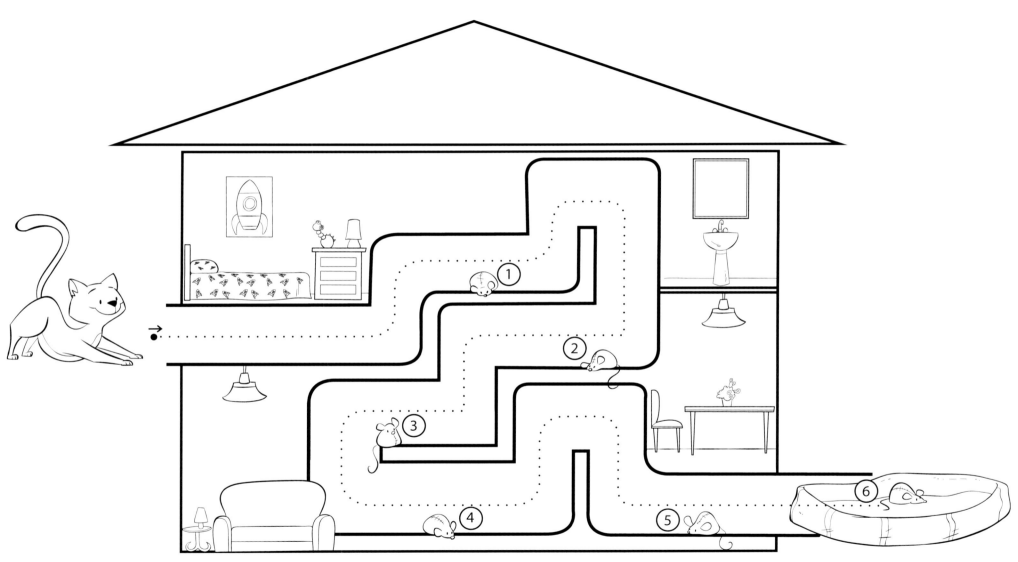

Colour and cut the pictures and words.

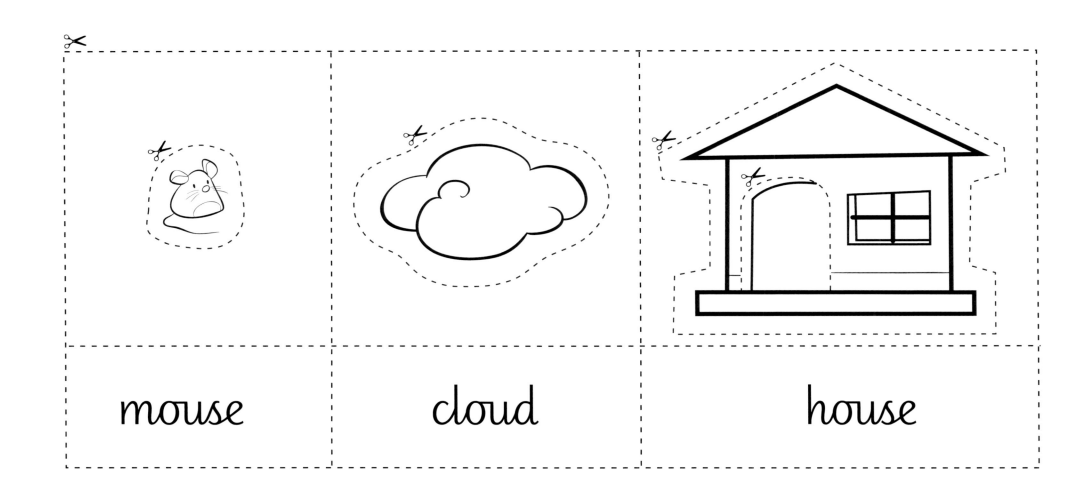

mouse

cloud

house

Autumn Fun!

Autumn project: Paint, cut and stick to make an autumn scene.

Autumn project: Paint, cut and stick to make an autumn scene.

3 Where Is Greenman?

Colour and trace. Then cut and play
Where is Greenman?

school   fire station   hospital

restaurant   playground   shop

Where is Greenman? / Is he in the (shop)? No he isn't. / Yes, he is. (restaurant, playground, hospital, school, fire station.)

Greenman and the Magic Forest B © Cambridge University Press. **Photocopiable 11**

Find and circle 5 differences. Then colour Greenman.

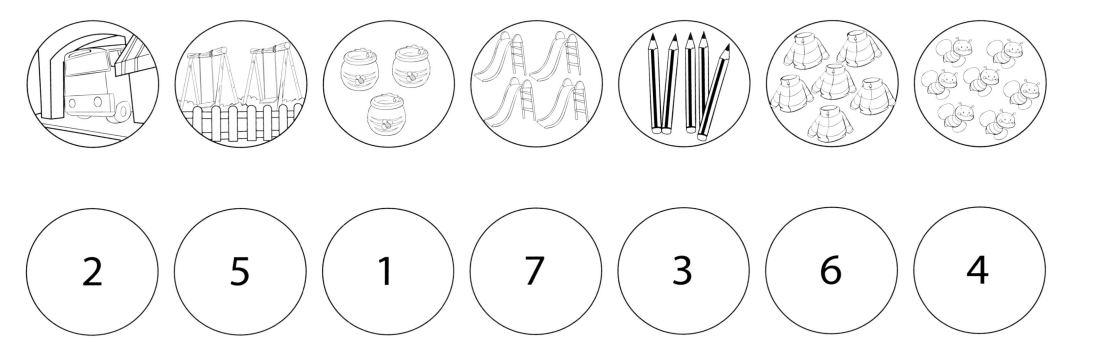

Colour and decorate.

We are stars!

4 The Loud Wind

Colour and trace. Then cut and play the *Can I have some…?* game.

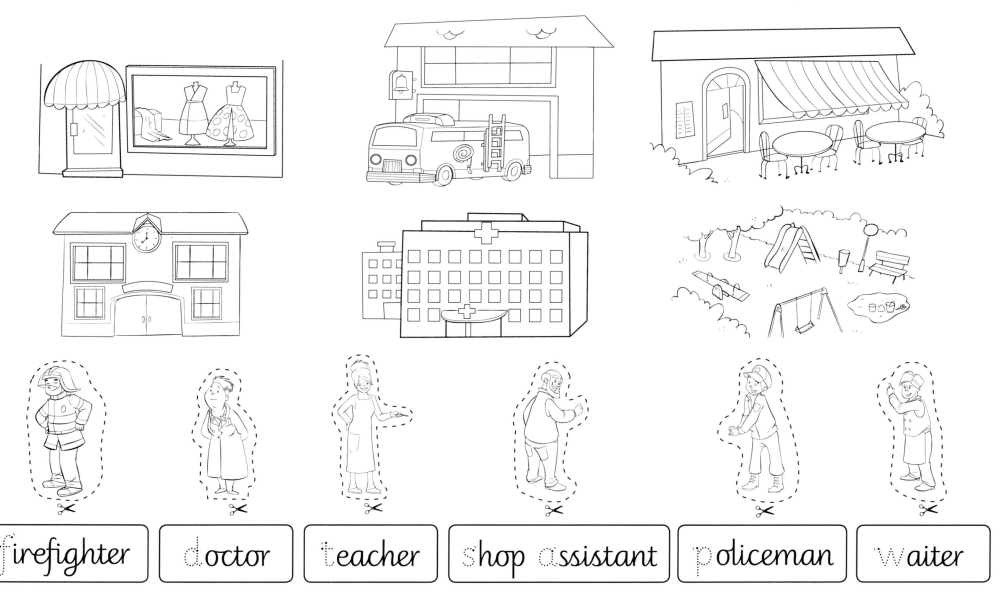

| firefighter | doctor | teacher | shop assistant | policeman | waiter |

Greenman and the Magic Forest B © Cambridge University Press. **Photocopiable 15**

Trace, count and match. Then make a wind chime.

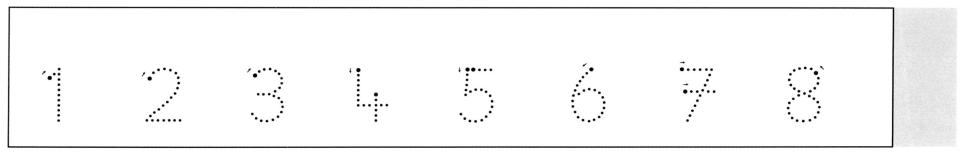

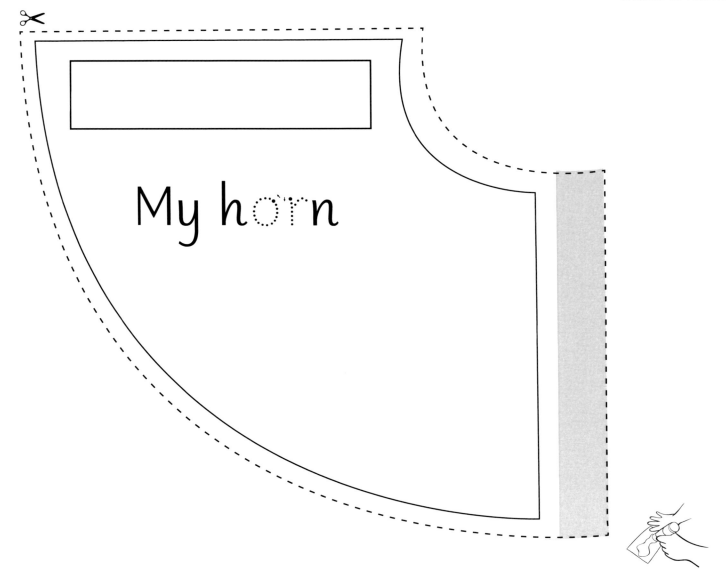

My horn

Winter Fun!

Winter project: Paint, cut and stick to make a winter scene.

Winter project: Paint, cut and stick to make a winter scene.

5 A Great Game

Match and trace. Then cut and play the *Who are you?* game.

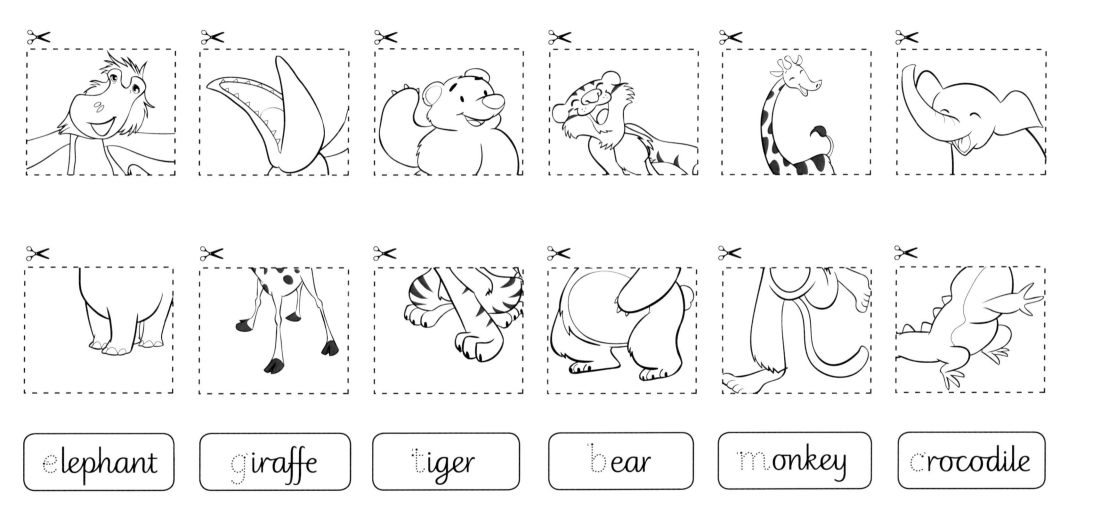

elephant giraffe tiger bear monkey crocodile

Find and circle 5 differences. Then colour Sam.

Join the numbers in order. Then colour.

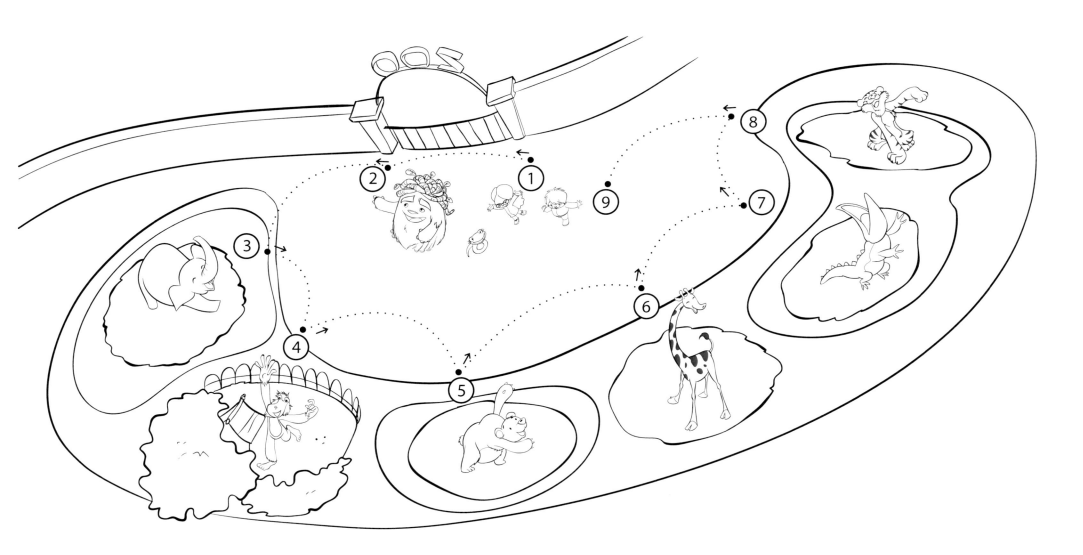

Play the *Vets and the zebra* game.

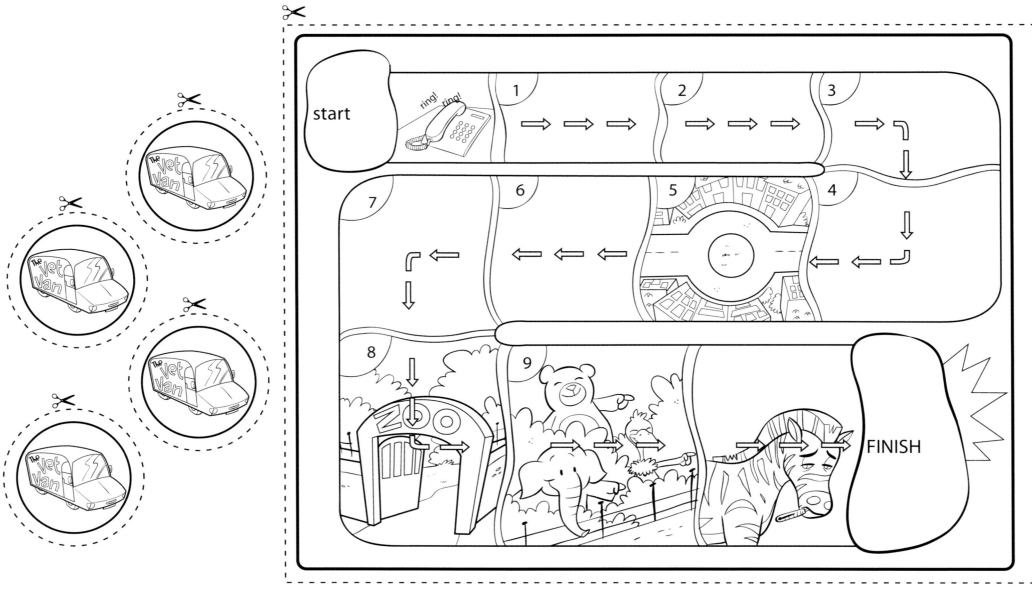

6 Rain Water

Follow and match. Then cut and play the *I like / I don't like* game.

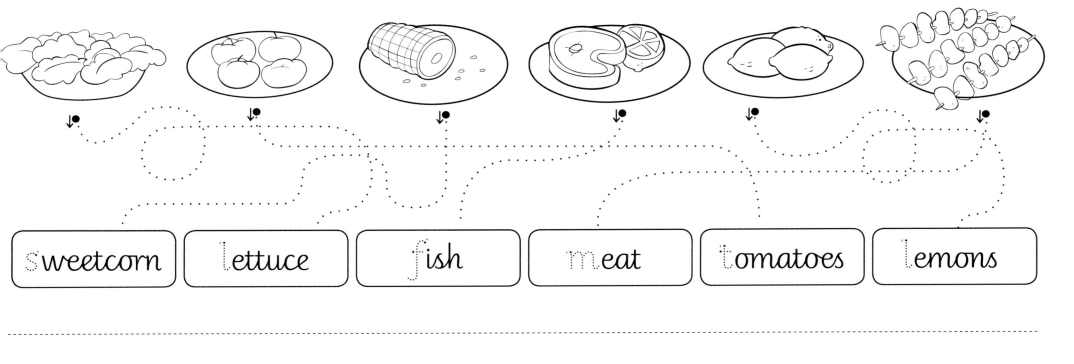

| sweetcorn | lettuce | fish | meat | tomatoes | lemons |

I like (fish). / I don't like (sweetcorn, lettuce, meat, tomato, lemon).

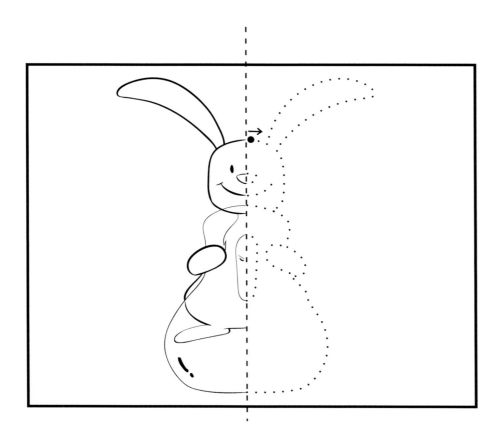

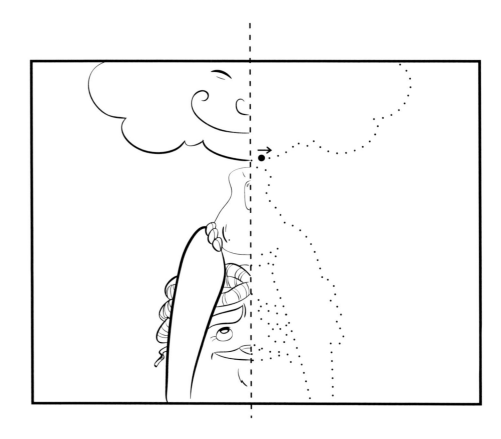

Trace your hands and number your fingers 1 - 10. Then move your 'fingers' and count to 10.

1	2	3
4	5	6
7	8	9
10		

thirsty	juice	thirsty	juice
thirsty	juice	thirsty	juice
thirsty	juice	thirsty	juice

Spring Fun!

Spring project: Paint, cut, stick and make your butterfly fly.

Greenman and the Magic Forest B © Cambridge University Press. **Photocopiables 29 and 30**

Spring project: Paint, cut and stick to make a hopping bunny.

■ Bunny

Summer Fun!

Summer project: Make and put on your summer hat.

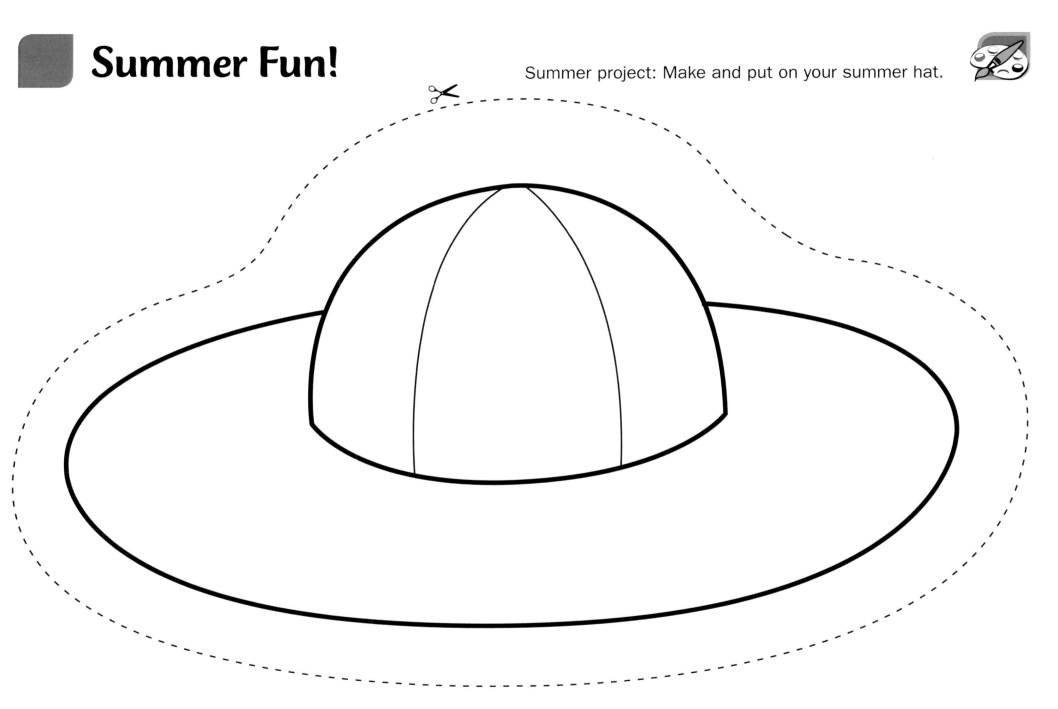

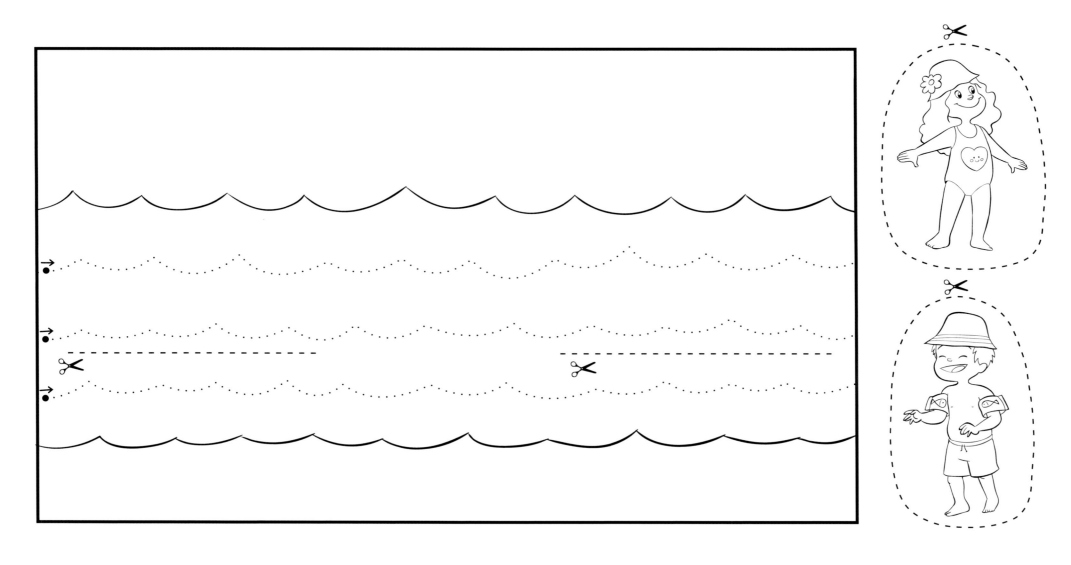

Congratulations!

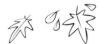

Name _____

Halloween

 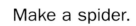

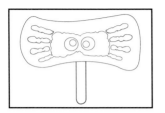

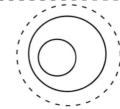

◼ Spider

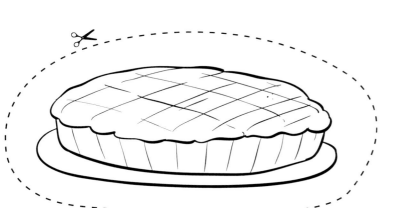

My pie

My bike

_____

_____

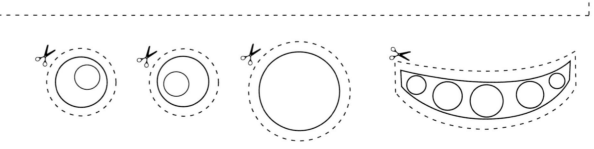

1 top

2 bike

3 kite

4 teddy

5 plane

6 coin

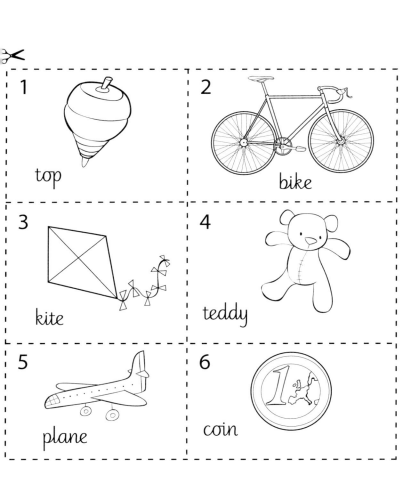

Toy box

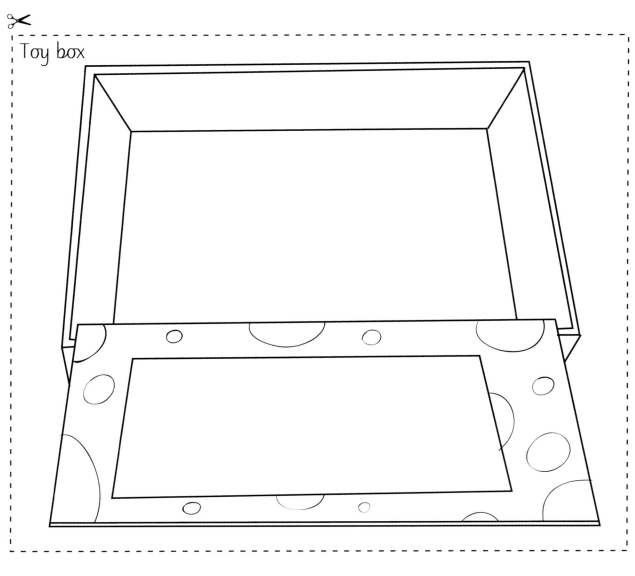

Easter

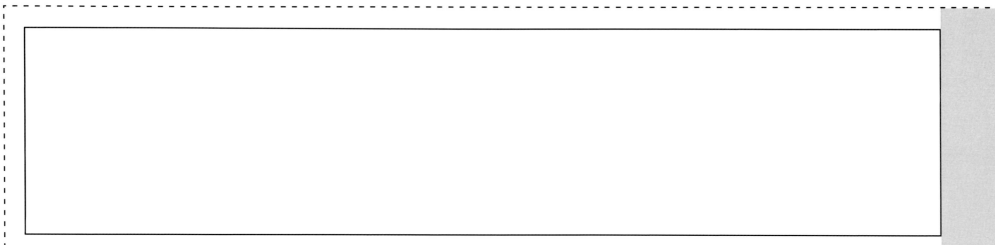

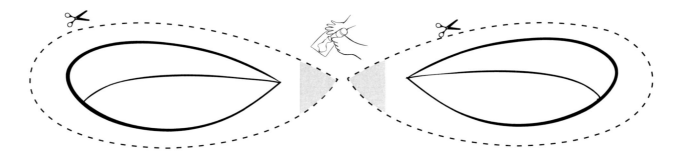

Cut out and play the *qu mime* game.

duck	queen	quick	quiet
duck	queen	quick	quiet
duck	queen	quick	quiet

Greenman and the Magic Forest B © Cambridge University Press. **Photocopiable 39**

Green Day

Make the Earth puzzle.

Colour and decorate 'My bird'.

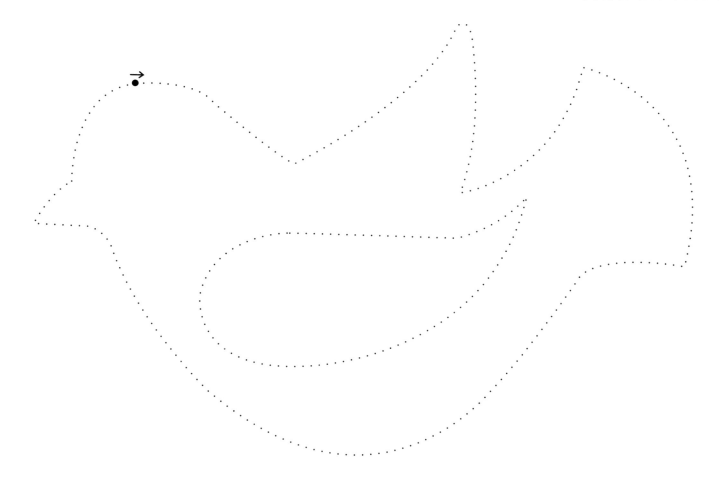

My bird

Goodbye!

Goodbye!

Goodbye!

CAMBRIDGE
UNIVERSITY PRESS

University Printing House, Cambridge CB2 8BS, United Kingdom

One Liberty Plaza, 20th Floor, New York, NY 10006, USA

477 Williamstown Road, Port Melbourne, VIC 3207, Australia

314–321, 3rd Floor, Plot 3, Splendor Forum, Jasola District Centre, New Delhi – 110025, India

103 Penang Road, #05-06/07, Visioncrest Commercial, Singapore 238467

José Abascal, 56–1°, 28003 Madrid, Spain

Cambridge University Press is part of the University of Cambridge.

It furthers the University's mission by disseminating knowledge in the pursuit of education, learning and research at the highest international levels of excellence.

www.cambridge.org
© Cambridge University Press 2015

First published 2015

20 19 18 17 16 15

Printed in Spain by Pulmen
Legal deposit: M-3627-2015

ISBN   978-84-9036-838-1   Teacher's Resource Book B
ISBN   978-84-9036-834-3   Pupil's Book B (with Stickers and Pop-outs)
ISBN   978-84-9036-835-0   Big Book B
ISBN   978-84-9036-836-7   Teacher's Book B
ISBN   978-84-9036-837-4   Guía Didáctica B
ISBN   978-84-9036-840-4   Flashcards B
ISBN   978-84-9036-839-8   Phonics Flashcards B
ISBN   978-84-9036-841-1   Wordcards B
ISBN   978-84-9036-842-8   Class Audio CDs B
ISBN   978-84-9036-843-5   Digital Forest B
ISBN   978-84-9036-845-9   Routine Board
ISBN   978-84-9036-000-2   Reward Stickers
ISBN   978-84-9036-001-9   Reward Stamp
ISBN   978-84-9036-846-6   Teacher's Bag
ISBN   978-84-9036-844-2   Puppet

Thanks and Acknowledgements

Author's thanks

Marilyn Miller would like to thank everyone at Cambridge University Press. In particular, to Jeannine Bogaard and Julieta Hernández for providing me with the opportunity to write, and to Mercedes Lopez de Bergara for her continued support.

Karen Elliott would like to thank everyone at Cambridge University Press and in particular Mercedes López de Bergara for her enthusiasm and dedication to the phonics section of the project; Mary Ockenden at the American School Bilbao, Aitziber Gutiérrez and Piluca Baselga at the Colegio Infantil Haurbaki for their help and suggestions on phonics at various stages of the project.

A special thank you goes to Juan González Cué, our Production Project Manager.

The authors and publishers are grateful to the following illustrators:

Gema García Ingelmo: cover illustration and characters concept
Antonio Cuesta Cornejo: illustration

The publishers are grateful to the following contributors:

Teresa del Arco: layout and design
Chefer: cover design

www.greenmanandthemagicforest.es

GREENMAN & THE MAGIC FOREST STARTER
GREENMAN & THE MAGIC FOREST A
▶ **GREENMAN & THE MAGIC FOREST B**

CAMBRIDGE
UNIVERSITY PRESS
www.cambridge.org

ISBN 978-84-9036-838-1

9 788490 368381